THE
DOLLAR WRITERS

This book is dedicated to:
YOU, The Dollar Reader

WELCOME TO THE FUTURE

Thanks for your order! This book is one part of our $5 Reader Series. Check that and the $1 Reader Series to change your life within 2 hours or less!

But first...

Scan the QR code below to dive deeper into the world of success!

The Dollar Writers

Get new updates and discounts to our products and services.

Your adventure with us has just begun.

Welcome aboard!

How-To Make Millions with Megabytes

Mastering the Strategies of Young Millionaires

Copyright © 2023

ISBN: 9798396658721

By: Our Team, The Dollar Writers

3D Radiance Publishing, LLC. All rights reserved.

Table of Contents

Table of Contents v

Disclaimer vi

Introduction vii

The First Million...ix

Understanding the Digital Landscape................. 1

Potential for Digital Wealth Creation................. 6

Identifying Profitable Niches and Markets.........13

Building an Online Presence 18

Creating Valuable Digital Products 23

Monetizing Digital Assets 29

Leveraging Technology and Automation...........35

Ethical and Social Business Practices...............40

Developing Digital Marketing Strategies...........45

The Final Wrap...60

Disclaimer

"The financial information provided in this book is for educational and informational purposes only. It is not intended as, and does not constitute, financial advice. The reader is solely responsible for any financial decisions they make based on the information in this book. The authors and/or publishers are not responsible for any financial loss or other damages that may result from the use of this book's content. Always consult a financial professional before making any significant financial decisions."

Introduction

"How-To Make Millions with Megabytes - Mastering the Strategies of Young Millionaires" is the second book in "The Five Dollar Reader Series" by The Dollar Writers. We are excited to share the strategies and techniques that young millionaires have used to create wealth and success in the digital landscape.

In today's world, digital technologies have revolutionized how we live, work, and do business. With the evolving climb of social media, the internet, and other digital platforms, countless opportunities exist to create wealth and build a successful business. However, many people struggle to master the digital strategies and skills necessary to succeed in this new landscape.

That's where this book comes in. "How-To Make Millions with Megabytes" is an excellent guide to mastering digital strategies and creating wealth in the digital age. Based on our principles of creating valuable content and prioritizing ethical and socially responsible business practices, this book provides actionable steps and strategies to help you succeed.

Throughout the book, you will learn how to understand and analyze the digital landscape, develop the mindset of a young millionaire, identify profitable niches and markets, build a solid online presence, create valuable digital products, monetize digital assets, leverage technology and automation, and maintain ethical and socially responsible business practices.

You can achieve financial success through digital strategies, regardless of your background or experience. By following the steps and strategies we provide here, you will be on your way to mastering the digital landscape and creating wealth in the digital age.

Thank you for choosing "How-To Make Millions with Megabytes - Mastering the Strategies of Young Millionaires" by The Dollar Writers. Be sure to check out The One Dollar Reader Series, our short and effective self-help books that will help you create a better self from within!

The First Million

As we enter the digital age, there are more and more new opportunities for wealth creation. From e-commerce to social media marketing, there are countless ways to leverage digital tools and platforms to create valuable products and services, build an online following, and generate significant revenue. However, mastering the strategies of young millionaires and achieving financial success requires more than just a basic understanding of digital technologies. It requires a strategic mindset, a commitment to consistent action, and a willingness to take calculated risks.

To make millions with megabytes, it is important to focus on creating value for your customers. This means identifying profitable niches and markets, developing deep insights into your target audience and their needs, and creating products and services that meet those needs in a valuable way. Also, it means staying up to date with emerging technologies and trends, and being willing to pivot and adapt in order to stay ahead of the competition.

One key strategy for making millions with megabytes is to build a strong online presence. This includes developing a professional and compelling website or online store, establishing a presence on social media, and creating valuable content that attracts and inspires your audience. It also means leveraging digital advertising and marketing strategies to reach a wider audience in order to drive conversions.

Another essential strategy is to leverage the power of data and analytics to make informed business decisions. Tracking metrics such as website traffic, customer engagement, and sales data, you can identify areas for improvement and make great decisions to optimize your business and maximize revenue. That includes staying up to date with the latest tools and technologies for data analysis and visualization, and developing a deep understanding of the insights and trends that drive business success.

In addition to these strategies, it is essential to develop a growth-oriented mindset and a willingness to take calculated risks. This means embracing failure and using it as a learning opportunity. It also means investing in your own personal and professional development, and surrounding yourself with like-minded individuals who share your vision and can support you on your journey to financial success.

Ultimately, the key to making millions with megabytes is to adopt a strategic mindset, commit to consistent action, and focus on creating value for your customers. Frequently follow emerging technologies and trends, leverage data and analytics to make informed decisions, and embrace failure as a learning opportunity. With this thought process, you can master the strategies of young millionaires and achieve financial success in the digital age.

Chapter 1:
Understanding the Digital Landscape

Introduction

In this chapter, we will provide information of the digital landscape, and explain the potential for wealth creation through digital strategies. We will also offer steps to analyze and understand the digital landscape to identify profitable opportunities. Understanding the digital landscape is crucial to identifying profitable opportunities and building a successful business. You can achieve financial success by adopting the right mindset and taking consistent action towards wealth creation.

As you begin your journey towards mastering digital strategies and creating wealth in the digital age, it is essential to understand how it is evolving. By staying up to date with emerging trends and key players, you can identify opportunities to create valuable products, build a strong online presence, and monetize digital assets.

Overview of the Digital Landscape

The digital landscape is a constantly evolving space that includes technologies and platforms. They enable individuals and businesses to create, share, and consume information and content. Some key trends and players in the digital landscape include:

1. Social media platforms like Facebook, Instagram, and Twitter (X)

2. E-commerce platforms such as Amazon, eBay, and Shopify

3. Streaming services such as Netflix, Hulu, and Spotify

4. Artificial intelligence and machine learning technologies

5. Virtual and augmented reality technologies

The potential for wealth creation through digital strategies is immense. By leveraging these technologies and platforms, individuals and businesses can create valuable content, build an online following, and monetize digital assets. However, it is important to approach it with a strategic mindset and identify profitable opportunities based on market research and analysis. With the rise of technology, it has transformed the way we communicate, work, and do business. Today, there are countless opportunities to create wealth and build a successful business through digital strategy.

Potential for Wealth Creation

Digital strategies have the potential to generate significant wealth and success for individuals and businesses. Using these technologies and platforms makes it possible to reach a global audience, connect with real customers, and generate revenue through various channels such as advertising, affiliate marketing, and product sales.

Analyze and Understand the Digital Landscape

To identify profitable opportunities in the digital landscape, it's important to conduct thorough research. Here are a few steps you could take to help you analyze and understand the digital landscape:

1. Conduct a bit of market research to help identify profitable niches and markets.

2. Monitor competitors and market conditions.

3. Analyze your competitors and identify gaps in the market.

4. Develop a deep understanding of your audience and their needs.

5. Understand customer behavior and preferences.

6. Identify opportunities to create valuable content and monetize digital assets.

Conclusion

In conclusion, understanding the digital landscape is essential for mastering digital strategies and creating wealth. We have provided you with actionable steps and strategies for analyzing and understanding the digital landscape to identify profitable opportunities. Remember to approach it with the mindset of prioritizing valuable content. By following these principles and the steps outlined in this chapter, you will be on your way to mastering the digital landscape and achieving financial success.

Chapter 2:
Potential for Digital Wealth Creation

Introduction

Welcome to Chapter 2 of "How-To Make Millions with Megabytes - Mastering the Strategies of Young Millionaires". In this chapter, we will explore the potential for creating wealth through digital strategies and provide actionable steps and strategies for unlocking your potential for success in the digital landscape.

The digital landscape offers countless opportunities for wealth creation and success. However, it is essential to unlock your full potential and leverage your unique strengths and passions to take advantage of these opportunities. In this chapter, we will provide detailed instructions and examples for identifying your strengths and passions, overcoming limiting beliefs and mindsets, and taking action towards creating wealth in the digital age.

Understanding Your Strengths and Passions

To unlock your potential for digital wealth creation, it is essential to understand your unique strengths and passions. By leveraging these strengths and passions, you can create valuable digital products and services that resonate with your target audience. Here are some detailed instructions and examples to help you identify your strengths and passions:

1. Personality assessments: We recommend taking a personality assessment such as the Myers-Briggs Type Indicator or even one called, StrengthsFinder. These assessments will provide you with a detailed report of your personality traits and strengths, which you can use to identify your unique strengths and passions.

2. Personal inventory: Conduct a personal inventory to identify your passions, interests,

and skills. This can involve creating a list of your hobbies and interests, reflecting on your past experiences and successes, and asking yourself what you enjoy doing and what you are good at.

3. Analyzing successes: Analyze your previous successes and accomplishments to identify the skills and attributes that contributed to your success. Ask yourself questions like "What was done well?" and "What strengths did I use to achieve this success?"

4. Seeking feedback: Seek feedback from others, such as colleagues or mentors, on your strengths and areas for improvement. Ask for specific examples of times when you demonstrated any particular strengths, and use this feedback to identify your unique strengths and passions.

Overcoming Limiting Beliefs and Mindsets

Limiting beliefs and mindsets can hold individuals back from achieving success in the digital landscape. These beliefs may include things like "I'm not good at computers" or "I don't have enough experience to succeed". To unlock your potential for digital wealth creation, it is essential to identify and overcome these limiting beliefs and mindsets. Read over some of these examples on how to do just that:

1. Mindfulness and self-awareness: As we mentioned in our One Dollar Reader Series, practice mindfulness and self-awareness to identify limiting beliefs and mindsets when they arise. Take a bit of time and reflect on your thoughts and feelings, and use this self-awareness to identify when negative self-talk or limiting beliefs are holding you back.

2. Seeking out mentors: Seek out role models and mentors who have achieved success in the digital landscape and learn from their experiences. Follow successful entrepreneurs on social media, read books and articles by successful digital entrepreneurs, and seek out mentorship opportunities in your community.

3. Taking action: Take action towards your goals, even in the face of setbacks or failures, and maintain a positive attitude towards success. Set SMART goals, break down goals into smaller steps, and build accountability systems to stay on track. (SMART) specific, measurable, attainable, realistic, and timebound.

Taking Action Towards Wealth Creation

To increase your potential for digital wealth creation, it is essential to take action towards your goals and implement digital strategies that align with your strengths and passions. Here are few ways you can take action towards wealth creation:

1. Creating a plan of action: Create a plan of action for achieving your digital wealth creation goals. Your plan should include specific steps and deadlines for achieving your goals, and should be broken down into manageable tasks.

2. Maximizing productivity: Maximize your productivity by using productivity apps and time management techniques. Use a productivity app like Trello or Asana to manage your tasks and deadlines, and use time management techniques to maximize your focus and productivity.

3. Feedback and analytics: Seek out feedback from your target audience and analyze analytics to make data-driven decisions about your digital products and services. Use customer feedback to improve your products and services, and track metrics like website traffic and social media engagement to identify areas for improvement.

4. Adapting and improving: Continuously adapt and improve your digital strategies based on feedback and market trends. Remember to stay up to date with any new trends and always incorporate customer feedback into your product development process. Focus on providing value to your target audience and staying ahead of the competition.

Conclusion

In conclusion, unlocking your potential for digital wealth creation requires a combination of self-awareness, action-taking, and strategic thinking. By identifying your unique strengths and passions, overcoming limiting beliefs and mindsets, and taking action towards your goals, you can create valuable digital products and services that resonate with your target audience and generate significant wealth.

Remember to stay focused on providing value to your target audience. Then keep adapting and improving your strategies based on feedback and analytics. Keeping these principles in mind, you can achieve success as a young millionaire in the digital landscape.

Chapter 3:
Identifying Profitable Niches and Markets

Introduction

In today's world, identifying profitable niches and markets is essential for creating successful digital products and services. In this chapter, we'll explore the importance of market research in identifying profitable niches and markets and provide actionable steps for readers to identify underserved markets and target profitable niches.

Identifying Profitable Niches and Markets

Before you begin creating digital products and services, it's important to conduct some market research and to identify profitable niches and markets. This research can help you understand the needs and preferences of your target audience, identify underserved markets, and position your products and services for success.

Thorough Market Research

There are several strategies for conducting thorough market research, here are a few:

1. Online surveys: Use online survey tools like SurveyMonkey or Google Forms to collect data from your target audience.

2. Social media listening: Use these social media listening tools like Hootsuite or Mention to monitor social media conversations related to your niche or market. This can help you understand what people are saying about your industry and identify areas for improvement.

3. Keyword research: Use keyword research tools like Google Keyword Planner or SEMrush to identify popular keywords related to your niche or market. This can help you

understand what people are searching for and identify potential gaps in the market.

Realize the importance of market research in identifying profitable niches and markets. By conducting this research, you can identify underserved markets and target profitable niches. This can help you create digital products and services that meet the needs of your audience and position yourself for success in a crowded market.

Identify Underserved Markets and Target Profitable Niches

Here are a few actionable steps to assist you with identifying underserved markets and target profitable niches:

1. Define your audience: Define your target audience and identify their needs, preferences, and pain points. This will help you create digital products and services that meet their needs and position yourself for success.

2. Thorough market research: Use the techniques and strategies we discussed earlier to conduct thorough market research and identify potential gaps in the market.

3. Analyze competition: Analyze your competition and identify areas where you can differentiate yourself and provide unique value to your target audience.

4. Niche-specific: Create a niche-specific value proposition that communicates the unique value you provide to your target audience.

Conclusion

In conclusion, conducting thorough market research is essential for identifying profitable niches and markets and positioning yourself for success in today's digital landscape. By defining your target audience, conducting thorough market research, analyzing your competition, and creating a niche-specific value proposition, you can identify underserved markets and target profitable niches. Remember to stay focused on providing value to your target audience and continuously adapting and improving your digital strategies based on feedback and analytics.

Chapter 4:
Building an Online Presence

Introduction

In this chapter, we'll explore the importance of building a strong online presence and provide strategies for creating and optimizing websites, social media profiles, and other digital assets. We'll also provide actionable steps for readers to develop a strong online presence and build a loyal following.

The Importance of Building a Strong Presence

A strong online presence is essential to help you establish credibility, help you build trust with your audience, and position your business for success. By creating and optimizing digital assets like websites and social media profiles, you can connect with your audience and build a loyal following.

Creating and Optimizing Websites

Here are some strategies for creating and optimizing websites, social media profiles, and other digital assets:

1. A consistent brand: Develop a consistent brand across all your digital assets to establish credibility and build trust with your audience. For example, use the same name, logo, color scheme, and tone of voice across your website and social media profiles.

2. Optimize: Optimize your website for search engines, ensuring that it's easy to navigate and user-friendly. This can help you gain more organic traffic and create new leads. For example, use keywords in your website copy, include meta descriptions and title tags, and make sure your website is mobile-friendly.

3. Engaging social media profiles: Create engaging social media profiles that reflect your brand's values and personality. Use high-quality visuals, engaging captions, and hashtags to attract followers and increase engagement. For example, use eye-catching images and videos, write captions that spark conversation, and use relevant hashtags to reach a wider audience. If you're a travel blogger, share stunning photos and videos of your adventures and write captions that inspire your audience to explore new places.

Strong Online Presence and Build a Loyal Following

Here are some actionable steps for developing a strong online presence and building a loyal following:

1. Define your brand: Start by defining your brand's values, personality, and unique selling proposition. This will help you create a consistent brand across all your digital assets. For example, if you're a fitness brand,

your values include health, wellness, and empowerment, and your unique selling proposition is personalized workout plans.

2. Develop a website: Develop a website that's optimized for search engines and user-friendly. Include valuable content that helps your audience solve problems and achieve their goals. For example, if you're a food blogger, create recipe posts and instructional videos that provide step-by-step guidance on how to cook delicious meals.

3. Provide valuable content: Provide valuable content on your website and social media profiles that helps your audience solve problems and achieve their goals. This can help you establish authority and build trust with your audience. For example, if you're a business consultant, create blog posts, eBooks, and webinars that provide practical advice on how to start and grow a successful business.

4. Engaging with your audience: Engage on social media with your audience, responding

to then and creating a sense of community around your brand. For example, if you're a beauty influencer, reply to comments and direct messages, ask your audience for feedback on your content, and share user-generated content to showcase your community. Also, host giveaways and contests to engage your audience.

Conclusion

Remember that building a strong online presence is essential for business success in today's digital landscape. By developing a consistent brand, creating, and optimizing websites, social media profiles, and other digital assets, providing valuable content, and engaging with your audience, you can develop a strong online presence and build a loyal following. Remember to stay focused on providing value to your audience and continuously adapting and improving your digital strategies based on feedback and analytics. By following these principles, you can establish a powerful presence online and grow to new heights with your business.

Chapter 5:
Creating Valuable Digital Products

Introduction

Creating valuable digital products is an effective way to build wealth and establish yourself as an expert in your field. Now, we'll explore the benefits of creating valuable digital products and provide techniques and strategies for creating and marketing digital products such as eBooks, courses, and online coaching. We'll also provide actionable steps for readers to create and launch profitable digital products.

The Benefits of Creating Valuable Products

Creating valuable digital products can provide several benefits, including:

1. Passive income: Digital products can generate passive income, allowing you to

make money when you're not actively working.

2. Increased authority: Creating valuable digital products can establish you as a legitimate authority in your field, and build your personal brand.

3. Scalability: Digital products can be scaled easily, allowing you to reach a wider audience without increasing your workload.

4. Flexibility: Digital products can be created and launched quickly and easily, providing flexibility and freedom in your work.

Creating and Marketing Digital Products

Here are some techniques and strategies for creating and marketing digital products:

1. Conduct a competitive analysis: Research your competition and identify what types of digital products they are offering. This will help you identify gaps in the market and find

opportunities to create unique and valuable products.

2. Create an outline: Creating an outline for your digital product will help you organize your thoughts and ensure that your product is structured in a way that is easy for your audience to follow.

3. Focus on solving a specific problem: Identify a specific problem that your audience has and create a digital product that provides a practical solution to that problem.

4. Create high-quality content: Your digital product's quality should be high, and provide value to your audience. Consider hiring a professional editor or designer to help you create a professional looking and well-polished product.

5. Offer bonuses and incentives: Consider offering bonuses or incentives to encourage your audience to purchase your digital product. This could include additional

resources, access to exclusive content, or one-on-one coaching.

Actionable Steps to Create and Launch Profitable Products

Here are some actionable steps for creating and launching profitable digital products:

1. Choose a profitable niche: Research your target audience and identify their needs. Use tools like Google Trends, social media, and online forums to gather insights and data.

2. Develop valuable content: Use your expertise and unique perspective to create valuable content that provides practical solutions to your target audience's pain points and needs. Consider creating a content calendar to stay organized and consistent.

3. Choose the right format: Choose the right format for your digital product based on your target audience's preferences and needs.

Consider creating an eBook, online course, or coaching program.

4. Use effective marketing strategies: Use effective marketing strategies such as social media, email marketing, and content marketing to promote your digital products. Consider creating a sales funnel that includes lead magnets, email sequences, and upsells.

5. Price your products appropriately: Price your digital products appropriately based on the value they provide and your target audience's budget. Consider offering different pricing tiers and payment options to make your products more accessible.

Conclusion

In conclusion, creating valuable digital products is a powerful way to build wealth and establish yourself as an expert in your field. By choosing a profitable niche, developing valuable content, choosing the right format, using effective marketing strategies, and pricing your products appropriately, you can create and launch profitable digital products that provide value to your audience and generate passive income. Remember to stay consistent with your goals and guidelines, prioritize your audience's satisfaction and needs, and continuously adapt.

Chapter 6:
Monetizing Digital Assets

Introduction

In this chapter, we'll explore the various ways to monetize digital assets and generate sustainable income streams. We'll provide an overview of the most common methods of digital monetization, such as advertising, affiliate marketing, and selling products and services. We'll also provide techniques and strategies for maximizing revenue through digital monetization and actionable steps for readers to monetize their own digital assets. We'll discuss how to choose the right monetization method, optimize digital assets for revenue, and build a loyal following to increase your influence and make it easier to monetize your digital assets.

Various Ways to Monetize Digital Assets

There are several ways to monetize digital assets, including:

1. Advertising: Advertising is a common way to monetize digital assets like websites, blogs, and social media channels. You can earn income by displaying ads on your digital assets and receiving payment based on clicks or impressions.

2. Affiliate marketing: This is a form of digital monetization where you earn a commission for promoting other people's products or services. You can promote these products and services through your digital assets such as a social media channel or blog, and earn commissions for resulting sales.

3. Selling products and services: You can monetize your digital assets by selling products and services. This can provide a sustainable income stream and allow you to establish yourself as an authority in your field.

Maximize Revenue Through Digital Monetization

Here are some techniques and strategies for maximizing revenue through digital monetization:

1. Choose the right method: Consider your target audience and their preferences to choose the right monetization method for your digital assets. Some examples include advertising, affiliate marketing, and selling products or services.

2. Optimize your monetization strategy: Once you've chosen your monetization method, optimize your strategy to maximize revenue. This could include optimizing ad placement and targeting, creating effective affiliate partnerships, or developing a product or service that meets a specific need in your niche.

3. Measure and improve: Continuously measure and improve your monetization strategy by analyzing data and adjusting your approach as needed. Use tools like Google Analytics or social media analytics to track your

performances and identify different areas for improvement.

Monetize Digital Assets and Generate Income

Here are some actionable steps for monetizing your digital assets and generating sustainable income streams:

1. Identify your monetization goals: Think about what you want to achieve through digital monetization, such as passive income or funding your business's growth. This will help you choose the right monetization methods and optimize your strategy.

2. Optimize your assets: Optimize your digital assets, such as your website or social media profiles, to maximize revenue. This could include improving your website's user experience, creating high-quality content, and optimizing your social media profiles for conversion.

3. Build a loyal following: Engage with your audience and provide value to build a loyal following. This can increase your influence and make it easier to monetize your digital assets. Consider tactics like email marketing, social media engagement, and content marketing.

4. Diversify income streams: Diversify your income streams by using multiple monetization methods. This can provide a more sustainable income stream and reduce your dependence on any one method. Consider using a mix of advertising, affiliate marketing, and selling products or services to create a well-rounded monetization strategy.

Conclusion

Maximizing revenue through digital monetization is a critical component of building a successful online business. As discussed, there are several ways to monetize digital assets and generate sustainable income streams. By choosing the right monetization methods, optimizing your digital assets, building a loyal following, and diversifying your income streams, you can maximize revenue and establish yourself as a legit authority or expert in your field. Remember to improve your digital monetization strategies based on feedback and analytics. Stay ethical and socially responsible in your monetization efforts, and always remember to prioritize providing value to your audience.

Chapter 7:
Leveraging Technology and Automation

Introduction

We have leveraged technology and automation in several of our books. It has allowed us to become more efficient and you can too. In this chapter, we'll explore the benefits of leveraging technology and automation for business success. We'll provide an overview of the most common technologies and tools that can help you automate tasks and optimize digital workflows. We'll also provide techniques and strategies for maximizing efficiency and growth through technology and actionable steps for readers to leverage technology and automation in their own businesses.

Leveraging Technology and Automation

There are several benefits to leveraging technology and automation, including:

1. Increased efficiency: Technology and automation can help you automate tasks and streamline workflows, which can save time and increase efficiency.

2. Improved accuracy: It can reduce the risk of human error and improve the accuracy of your processes.

3. Scalability: It also can help you scale your business by allowing you to handle more tasks and customers without adding more staff.

Automating Tasks and Optimizing Digital Workflows

Here are some techniques and strategies for automating tasks and optimizing digital workflows:

1. Identify repetitive tasks: Identify repetitive tasks in your business that can be

automated, such as email marketing or social media scheduling.

2. Choose the right tools: Choose the right tools for automation based on your business needs and budget. There are several automation tools available, such as Zapier or If This Then That (IFTTT), that can help you automate tasks.

3. Create efficient workflows: Create efficient workflows by mapping out your business processes and identifying areas for improvement. Use automation tools to streamline these processes and improve efficiency.

Leverage Technology for Business

Here are some actionable steps for leveraging technology and automation for business growth and efficiency:

1. Identify areas for automation: Identify areas in your business that can be automated using technology and tools.

2. Choose the right tools: Choose the right tools and the right software, based on your budget and your business needs.

3. Develop SOPs: Develop standard operating procedures for your business processes and tasks to ensure consistency and efficiency.

4. Train team members: Train team members on new technology and tools to ensure they are utilized properly and efficiently.

5. Leverage artificial intelligence (AI): Leverage AI tools and technologies, such as chatbots or machine learning, to automate customer service and improve customer engagement.

Conclusion

In conclusion, leveraging technology and automation can help you increase efficiency, improve accuracy, and scale your business. By identifying repetitive tasks, choosing the right tools, creating efficient workflows, and leveraging AI, you can automate tasks and optimize digital workflows for growth and efficiency. Remember to stay consistent with your goals and guidelines, prioritize your audience's satisfaction and needs, and continuously adapt and improve your technology and automation strategies based on feedback and analytics.

Chapter 8:
Ethical and Social Business Practices

Introduction

In this chapter, we'll explore the importance of ethical and social business practices in the digital landscape. We'll provide an overview of the most common ethical and social issues that businesses face and tips and strategies for maintaining transparency, sustainability, and other ethical standards. We'll also provide actionable steps for readers to build a socially responsible business that positively impacts the world.

The Importance of Ethical and Socially Responsible Practices

Ethical and socially responsible business practices are crucial for several reasons, including:

1. Building trust: Consumers are more likely to trust and support businesses that prioritize ethical and socially responsible practices.

2. Long-term sustainability: Ethical and socially responsible practices can help businesses build long-term sustainability and avoid negative consequences such as legal or reputational risks.

3. Positive impact on society: Businesses that prioritize social responsibility can have a positive impact on society by contributing to important causes and promoting positive change.

Maintaining Ethical and Responsible Practices

Here are some tips and strategies for maintaining ethical and socially responsible practices:

1. Prioritize transparency: Be transparent about your business practices and policies, such as data privacy and sustainability efforts.

2. Encourage diversity and inclusion: Prioritize diversity and inclusion in your hiring practices and create a welcoming and inclusive work environment.

3. Promote sustainability: Implement sustainable practices such as reducing waste and emissions, and sourcing materials responsibly.

Build a Socially Responsible Business with Positive Impact

Here are some actionable steps for building a socially responsible business that positively impacts the world:

1. Code of Ethics: Develop a Code of Ethics that outlines your commitment to ethical and socially responsible business practices. Ensure that all employees understand and adhere to this code.

2. Clear Communication: Establish clear communication channels with your customers, stakeholders, and employees. Encourage them to provide feedback on your business practices and use this feedback to improve.

3. Embrace Social Responsibility: Embrace Corporate Social Responsibility (CSR) by taking actions that positively impact society and the environment. Consider implementing sustainable practices, volunteering with local organizations, and supporting causes that align with your business values.

4. Support Suppliers: Partner with suppliers that prioritize ethical and socially responsible practices. Consider conducting audits or assessments to ensure that suppliers adhere to your standards.

Conclusion

In conclusion, maintaining ethical and socially responsible business practices is crucial for building trust with customers, ensuring long-term sustainability, and having a positive impact on society. By prioritizing transparency, diversity and inclusion, sustainability, and community involvement, you can build a socially responsible business that positively impacts the world. Remember to conduct thorough market research, create high-quality and engaging content, and continuously adapt and improve your business practices based on feedback and analytics.

Chapter 9:
Developing Digital Marketing Strategies

Introduction

Today, any company wishing to flourish in the internet world must have a strong digital marketing plan. Digital marketing refers to any marketing initiatives that reach out to potential customers using digital channels like social media, email, search engines, and websites. This chapter will examine the essential elements of a successful digital marketing strategy and offer practical techniques for developing and carrying out a successful digital marketing strategy.

Evaluate and Adjust

It is crucial to frequently assess the success of your digital marketing plan and make any necessary adjustments. It may be necessary to study statistics like website traffic, conversion rates, and your social media engagement insights for this. By regularly monitoring and adjusting your strategy, you can optimize it for maximum effectiveness and ensure that it is aligned with your business goals.

Trends and Technologies

The digital landscape is continually changing, with new platforms and technology appearing frequently. It's crucial to keep up with new trends and technology in the field of digital marketing if you want to stay ahead and keep your competitive advantage. This can entail participating in trade shows and conferences, reading trade journals, and networking with other industry experts.

Create a Budget

Digital marketing can demand a major time and resource commitment, so it is significant to create a budget and allocate resources effectively. This can involve hiring skilled professionals, investing in paid advertising, and leveraging automation tools to streamline processes and improve efficiency. By effectively allocating your resources, you can fulfil your business objectives and maximize the impact of your digital marketing initiatives.

Optimal Digital Marketing Plan

1. Recognizing your target market: Knowing your target audience is the first step in creating a successful digital marketing strategy. This involves figuring out their characteristics, passions, problems, and online habits. By Recognizing your target market, you can modify your marketing and messaging strategies to appeal to them and boost engagement.

2. Setting clear goals: Once you have identified your target market, it's important to set clear goals for your digital marketing efforts. These objectives must be SMART, or specific, measurable attainable, realistic, and timebound. Increased internet traffic, lead generation, sales, or improved brand recognition are a few examples of goals.

3. Developing a strong brand presence: This is critical for building trust with potential customers. This includes developing consistent branding, messaging, and visual design across your website, social media profiles, email marketing, and other digital channels.

4. Creating valuable content: Any successful digital marketing plan must include the creation of useful content. This includes developing content that educates, informs, or entertains your target audience. Blog entries, videos, infographics, social media posts, and email newsletters are a few examples of content.

5. Utilizing social media: Social media has the potential to be an effective tool for reaching out to potential clients and raising brand awareness. It's critical to determine the social media channels most appropriate for your target market and to create a plan that

supports your overall objectives for digital marketing.

6. Using SEO: SEO, or search engine optimization, is the process of improving the content of your website and how well it performs in search engine results pages (SERPs). You may improve organic site traffic, produce more leads and sales, and increase your website's visibility in search engine results.

7. Using compensated advertising: Paid advertisements, such as those found on Google Ads or in social media, can be a useful strategy for getting in front of your target market and generating leads and sales. Creating a clear advertising strategy that complements your overall digital marketing objectives and spending plan is crucial.

Actionable Steps for Creating a Successful Digital Marketing Plan

1. Identify your target market: To determine the needs of your target market, do out market research, demographics, interests, pain points, and online behaviors.

2. Set clear goals: For your digital marketing initiatives, Make SMART goals— specific, measurable, attainable, realistic, and timebound—for your organization.

3. Develop a strong brand presence: Develop consistent branding, messaging, and visual design across your website, social media profiles, email marketing, and other digital channels.

4. Create valuable content: Develop valuable content that educates, informs, or entertains your target audience.

5. Leverage social media: Identify the social media platforms that are the most relevant to your target audience and develop a strategy that aligns with your overall digital marketing goals.

6. Make use of search engine optimization: To improve organic traffic to your website, optimize both your website and its content for search engines.

7. Utilize paid advertising: Develop a clear advertising strategy that aligns with your overall digital marketing goals and budget.

8. Monitor and adjust: Monitor your digital marketing efforts regularly and adjust the strategy as needed. Base it on performance data and feedback from your target.

Identify Your Target Audience

Finding your target demographic is one of the most crucial steps in creating an effective digital marketing strategy. knowing the requirements of your target audience, preferences, and behavior is essential to creating content that resonates with them and drives conversions. Here are some steps to identify your target audience:

1. Carry out market analysis: Conduct market research to classify your target market, demographics, psychographics, and behavior. Use tools like Google Analytics and your social media insights to gather this data.

2. Create customer personas: Create customer personas that represent your target audience's needs, preferences, and behavior. You will use these to guide your content creation and marketing strategy.

3. Analyze customer feedback: Analyze customer feedback to understand their pain points and needs. Use this feedback to create content that provides practical solutions and resonates through target market.

Produce Interesting Content

1. An effective digital marketing strategy must include the development of interesting content. Engaging content may increase website traffic, improve your online visibility,

and produce leads and sales. These are some guidelines for producing interesting content:

2. Use visuals: Use visuals like images and videos, and even infographics to make your content more engaging and shareable.

3. Provide value: Provide value to your target audience by creating content that identifies their pain points while providing those practical solutions.

4. Keep it concise: Keep your content brief and to-the-point. Online audiences have short attention spans and are more likely to engage with content that is easy to consume.

Make use of social media

Social networking is an effective technique for contacting your target audience and developing a strong online presence. You can leverage social media as part of your digital marketing plan by using the following advice:

1. Select the appropriate platforms: Decide on the social media channels where your target market is most active.

2. Create engaging content: Create shareable, valuable material that appeals to your target audience.

3. Get your audience involved: Respond to their messages and comments, and take part in online debates to interact with your audience.

Improve Your Website's Search Engine Optimization

Building your online profile and generating organic traffic both depend on your website being optimized for search engines. Here are some pointers for making your website search engine-friendly:

1. Carry out a keyword search: To find any terms and phrases that your audience is looking for, use that keyword research.

Include these words in all of the text on your website.

2. Use metadata: Use metadata like title tags and meta descriptions to provide the search engines with lots of information about your website content.

3. Boost website speed: Boost website speed by optimizing images and minimizing unnecessary plugins.

Actionable Steps to Develop an Effective Digital Marketing Strategy

The following are some practical measures for creating a successful digital marketing strategy:

1. Determine who your target market: Conduct market research and create customer personas to identify your target audience.

2. Create engaging content: Create content that is valuable, concise, and engaging.

3. Leverage social media: Choose the right platforms, create engaging content, and engage with your audience.

4. Optimize your website for search engines: Use metadata and improve site speed.

You must carry out search engine optimization, or SEO, to elevate the position of your web page on search engine outcomes pages (SERPs). Your website can receive more organic visitors by placing higher in search results, which may improve conversions and income.

Keyword research, which entails figuring out the words and phrases your target market uses to look for goods or services connected to your company, is a crucial component of SEO. You will increase your chances of appearing higher in search results for these keywords by adding these keywords into the content and metadata of your website.

Link building, which is encouraging other websites to link back to your website, is another crucial component of SEO. As a result, your website may rank better in search results due to an increase in authority and reliability in the eyes of search engines.

Another successful digital marketing tactic is pay-per-click (PPC) advertising, which is posting adverts on social media or search engine platforms and getting paid for each click. With pay-per-click advertising, you can target specific keywords or demographics to reach your desired audience and increase conversions.

Platforms for social media marketing provide you the chance to interact with and establish relationships with your target market. By creating valuable content and engaging with your followers, you can increase brand awareness and loyalty. You will even drive traffic to your website and increase conversions.

Email marketing, which comprises sending promotional emails to your subscribers, is another effective digital marketing strategy. By providing valuable content and offers, you can build relationships with your subscribers and increase conversions.

In a more recent digital marketing method called influencer marketing, you collaborate with influencers or celebrities to push your goods or services to their following. You may boost brand recognition and credibility while also boosting sales and revenue by making use of the influencer's network and reputation.

Finally, data analysis and optimization are essential aspects of effective digital marketing. By tracking and analyzing your marketing metrics, such as website traffic, engagement, and conversion rates, you can pinpoint problem areas and tweak your marketing tactics to get the best results.

Conclusion

In order to establish a strong online presence and increase conversions, an effective digital marketing strategy must be created. By identifying your target audience and by following the steps outlined in this chapter, you can design a thorough digital marketing strategy that is adapted to your company's objectives and target market. With the right mindset, persistence, and consistent effort, you can achieve success and achieve your business goals through digital marketing.

The Final Wrap

As we come to the conclusion of this book, it is important to reflect on the journey we have taken and the knowledge we have gained about digital wealth creation. We have explored various strategies and techniques for building a successful digital business, from identifying profitable niches and markets to leveraging technology and automation. We have discussed the importance of maintaining ethical and socially responsible practices, and how to develop effective digital marketing strategies.

Now, as we look forward to the future, it is important to remember that the digital landscape is constantly evolving. Emerging technologies and platforms will continue to shape the way we do business, and new opportunities for wealth creation will arise. To continue to be innovative, it is essential to adopt a growth mindset and embrace lifelong learning.

One key area to focus on in the future is the intersection of technology and sustainability.

Businesses need to embrace sustainable practices and reduce their environmental impact as we continue to struggle with the global issues of climate change and resource depletion. By leveraging technology and innovation, it is possible to create sustainable solutions that benefit both the planet and the bottom line.

Another important trend to watch is the rise of artificial intelligence and machine learning. These new technologies have great potential to revolutionize the way we do business. From automating repetitive tasks to creating personalized customer experiences, it can work out for all those involved. By staying up to date with emerging trends and experimenting with new technologies, businesses can position themselves for long-term success.

Ultimately, the key to digital wealth creation is to be agile, adaptable, and focused on creating value for your customers. By consistently providing high-quality products and services, building a strong online presence, and maintaining ethical and socially responsible practices, you can create a sustainable and profitable digital business.

As you embark on your own journey towards digital wealth creation, remember to stay focused, stay curious, and stay true to your values. The road may be tough, long, and challenging, but with the right mindset and a continuous commitment to lifelong learning, you can achieve success beyond your wildest dreams. Thank you for joining us on this incredible journey, and best of luck in all your future endeavors.

Conclusion

Congratulations, you've just learned how to make millions with megabytes by mastering the strategies of young millionaires! We've covered a lot of ground. From understanding the digital landscape, developing a growth mindset, identifying profitable niches and markets, building an online presence, creating valuable digital products, monetizing digital assets, and leveraging technology and automation.

By mastering these strategies, you have the potential to create wealth and build a successful business in today's digital landscape. As we always mention throughout our books, it's crucial to keep in mind that success takes time. It takes consistent effort, hard work, and a commitment to learning and improving.

We encourage you to take action and implement the strategies discussed in this book. Start by conducting thorough market research, developing a growth mindset, building a strong online presence, creating valuable digital products, monetizing digital assets, and leveraging technology and automation. Remember to maintain ethical and socially responsible business practices to build trust with customers and positively impact society.

In conclusion, we want to emphasize the value of mastering digital strategies for creating wealth and building a successful business. We recommend reading our other how-to and self-help books to continue learning and improving. And always remember to stay consistent with our principles and guidelines, foster strong relationships with readers, and continuously adapt and improve based on feedback and analytics. Thank you for being a Dollar Reader and taking the first step towards financial success and personal growth.

"Let us help you make your first million dollars!"

Follow us on social media for special discounts and updates!

@DOLLARWRITERS

Loved what you read? Tell the world! We love hearing from our readers!

www.ingramcontent.com/pod-product-compliance
Lightning Source LLC
La Vergne TN
LVHW051605050326
832903LV00033B/4377